Table Of Contents

Chapter 1: Understanding ABDL Boundaries

Defining ABDL Boundaries

In this subchapter, we will delve into the crucial aspect of establishing and understanding ABDL boundaries. For family members of ABDL individuals, navigating these boundaries can be a challenging task. However, with open communication and a respectful attitude, it is possible to foster a healthy and supportive relationship with your ABDL loved one.

First and foremost, it is essential to recognize that ABDL boundaries are highly individual and can vary greatly from person to person. What may be acceptable or enjoyable for one ABDL individual may not be the same for another. Therefore, it is crucial to engage in open and non-judgmental conversations to understand their unique needs and desires.

The key to establishing healthy ABDL boundaries lies in open communication. Encourage your loved one to express their wants and needs openly, without fear of judgment or embarrassment. By actively listening and showing empathy, you can create a safe space for them to share their thoughts, preferences, and limits.

It is equally important to voice your own boundaries and concerns as a family member. While it is essential to support your loved one's ABDL identity, it is also crucial to ensure that your own boundaries are respected. Openly discussing your comfort levels and setting clear expectations will foster a balanced and respectful relationship.

Respecting privacy is another vital aspect of navigating ABDL boundaries. Understand that your loved one may need personal space and time to engage in their ABDL activities. It is crucial to honor their privacy and not invade their personal boundaries. Establishing trust and understanding will help maintain a healthy dynamic between you and your ABDL loved one.

Remember, acceptance and understanding are key in navigating ABDL boundaries. While it may be challenging at times, it is crucial to approach the topic with empathy and an open mind. Educate yourself about ABDL identity, seek resources, and engage in open dialogue with your loved one. By fostering a positive environment and showing support, you can strengthen your relationship and create a safe space for your ABDL family member.

In conclusion, defining ABDL boundaries requires open communication, empathy, and respect. By actively engaging in conversations, respecting privacy, and setting clear expectations, you can navigate these boundaries successfully. Remember, your loved one's ABDL identity is a part of who they are, and with acceptance and understanding, you can foster a supportive and healthy relationship.

Recognizing the Importance of Boundaries in ABDL Relationships

Introduction:

In any relationship, boundaries play a crucial role in establishing healthy dynamics and maintaining respect between individuals. This is no different when it comes to ABDL (Adult Baby/Diaper Lover) relationships. Understanding and acknowledging the importance of boundaries is essential for family members of ABDL individuals to create a supportive and nurturing environment. This subchapter aims to explore the significance of boundaries in ABDL relationships and provide guidance for family members on how to navigate and establish open communication.

Understanding Boundaries:

Boundaries are personal limits that help individuals feel safe, secure, and respected in their relationships. In the context of ABDL relationships, it is vital for family members to recognize and respect the boundaries set by their ABDL loved ones. These boundaries can vary greatly from person to person and may encompass aspects such as privacy, personal space, and emotional needs.

Establishing Open Communication:

Open communication is the key to navigating ABDL boundaries successfully. Family members should encourage their loved ones to express their needs, desires, and limitations openly. This includes creating a safe space for discussions, actively listening without judgment, and striving to understand their ABDL loved one's perspective.

Respecting Privacy:

Privacy is an essential aspect of ABDL relationships. Family members should respect their loved one's need for privacy and ensure that their personal ABDL activities and preferences remain confidential, unless the individual chooses to share them. This respect for privacy helps foster trust and creates an environment where the ABDL individual feels comfortable expressing their true selves.

Setting Clear Expectations:

Establishing clear expectations is crucial in ABDL relationships. Family members should openly discuss their own boundaries and expectations while also allowing their ABDL loved one to share theirs. This open dialogue ensures that both parties are aware of each other's limits, leading to a more fulfilling and respectful relationship.

Conclusion:

Recognizing the importance of boundaries in ABDL relationships is fundamental for family members to support their loved ones. By understanding and respecting the boundaries set by ABDL individuals, family members can foster an environment of open communication, empathy, and acceptance. Establishing clear expectations and respecting privacy are integral aspects of maintaining a healthy and respectful relationship. By navigating boundaries with sensitivity and understanding, family members can create a positive and nurturing environment for their ABDL loved one, promoting their overall well-being and happiness.

Common Misconceptions and Stereotypes about ABDL

In our society, there are often misconceptions and stereotypes surrounding the Adult Baby/Diaper Lover (ABDL) community. These misconceptions can lead to misunderstandings and strained relationships between ABDL individuals and their families. It is essential for family members to educate themselves and challenge these stereotypes to establish open communication and maintain a healthy and respectful relationship with their ABDL loved one.

One common misconception about ABDL is that it is purely a sexual fetish. While there may be a sexual component for some individuals, this is not the case for everyone. ABDL is a complex identity that encompasses a range of emotions, desires, and needs. It is essential to understand that ABDL is more than just a fetish and can provide comfort, stress relief, and a sense of identity for many individuals.

Another misconception is that ABDL individuals are regressing to an infantile state or attempting to relive their childhood. In reality, ABDL is about embracing a different side of oneself and exploring feelings of vulnerability, nurturing, and comfort. It is crucial to recognize that ABDL individuals are still adults with responsibilities and capabilities outside of their ABDL identity.

Stereotypes often portray ABDL individuals as mentally unstable or lacking maturity. This is far from the truth. ABDL individuals can be successful professionals, loving parents, and contributing members of society. It is crucial to separate the ABDL identity from an individual's overall character and judge them based on their actions and accomplishments, rather than their ABDL interests.

Lastly, there is a misconception that ABDL is inherently harmful or unnatural. It is important to understand that ABDL is a consensual and harmless lifestyle choice for those who engage in it. As long as it is practiced responsibly and within appropriate boundaries, it can bring joy and fulfillment to ABDL individuals' lives.

To establish open communication and foster a positive environment for your ABDL loved one, it is crucial to challenge these misconceptions and stereotypes. Educate yourself about ABDL by reading books, articles, and joining support groups or online communities. Engage in open and non-judgmental conversations with your loved one to understand their experiences, needs, and boundaries. Treat their ABDL identity with respect and acceptance, just as you would with any other aspect of their life.

By challenging misconceptions and stereotypes, you can create a supportive and inclusive environment for your ABDL loved one. Remember, empathy, understanding, and open communication are the keys to maintaining a healthy and respectful relationship with your ABDL family member.

Chapter 2: Navigating ABDL Boundaries

Establishing Open Communication with Your ABDL Loved One

Open communication is the foundation of any healthy and respectful relationship. When it comes to navigating the world of ABDL boundaries, it becomes even more crucial to establish open lines of communication with your ABDL loved one. In this subchapter, we will explore effective strategies and tips to help family members connect, understand, and support their ABDL loved ones.

1. Create a Safe Space: It is essential to create an environment where your ABDL loved one feels safe and comfortable discussing their feelings and desires. Make it clear that you are open to listening without judgment. Assure them that their thoughts and emotions are valid and that you are there to support them.

2. Active Listening: To establish open communication, practice active listening. This involves giving your full attention, maintaining eye contact, and responding without interruption. Show genuine interest in understanding their perspective and avoid dismissing their thoughts or feelings.

3. Empathy and Understanding: Empathy is key to fostering a positive environment. Put yourself in their shoes and try to understand their experiences, desires, and struggles. This will help you build a stronger connection and bridge any gaps in understanding.

4. Educate Yourself: Take the initiative to educate yourself about ABDL identities and the community. Understanding the terminology, motivations, and challenges faced by ABDL individuals will enable you to communicate more effectively and offer the support they need.

5. Respect Boundaries: Establishing and respecting boundaries is crucial for any relationship, particularly when it comes to ABDL. Have an open conversation about boundaries, discussing what is comfortable and what is not. This will help both parties understand each other's limits and ensure a healthy and respectful relationship.

6. Encourage Open Dialogue: Encourage your loved one to share their thoughts, feelings, and experiences openly. Create opportunities for dialogues by asking open-ended questions and actively engaging in discussions. This will help them feel heard and valued.

7. Seek Professional Guidance: If you find it challenging to establish open communication or encounter significant roadblocks, consider seeking professional guidance. Therapists or counselors specializing in ABDL issues can provide valuable insights and strategies to enhance communication and understanding.

Remember, establishing open communication is an ongoing process that requires patience, empathy, and understanding. By creating a safe and respectful environment, actively listening, and educating yourself, you can navigate ABDL boundaries with your loved one more effectively and foster a stronger, healthier relationship.

Creating a Safe and Non-Judgmental Space for Dialogue

In this subchapter, we will explore the importance of creating a safe and non-judgmental space for dialogue between family members and their ABDL loved ones. Open communication is vital to maintaining a healthy and respectful relationship, and it begins with establishing an environment where everyone feels safe to express themselves without fear of judgment or ridicule.

1. Recognizing the Need for a Safe Space:
Understanding the unique challenges that ABDL individuals face is crucial in

creating a safe space for dialogue. As a family member, it is essential to acknowledge your loved one's ABDL identity and the significance it holds for them. By doing so, you can demonstrate your willingness to listen and learn, fostering an environment of acceptance and understanding.

2. Practicing Active Listening:
Active listening involves fully engaging with the speaker, giving them your undivided attention, and responding in a non-judgmental manner. When engaging in a dialogue with your ABDL loved one, actively listen to their thoughts, feelings, and experiences. Validate their emotions and let them know that you hear them without interrupting or imposing your own beliefs.

3. Respecting Boundaries:
Respecting boundaries is crucial in creating a safe space for dialogue. Each individual has their own comfort levels and limits, and it is important to recognize and honor them. Allow your loved one to share as much or as little as they feel comfortable with, and refrain from prying or pressuring them into disclosing more than they are ready to share.

4. Cultivating Empathy and Understanding:
Empathy and understanding are essential in fostering a positive environment. Try to put yourself in your loved one's shoes and see the world from their perspective. Educate yourself about ABDL identity and the challenges they may face. By doing so, you can develop a deeper understanding and empathy for their experiences, which will ultimately strengthen your relationship.

5. Seeking Professional Help:
Sometimes, creating a safe space for dialogue may require the assistance of a professional. If you find yourselves struggling to establish open communication or if tensions arise, consider seeking the guidance of a therapist or counselor who specializes in ABDL-related issues. They can provide valuable insights and help facilitate constructive conversations.

In conclusion, creating a safe and non-judgmental space for dialogue is essential in maintaining a healthy and respectful relationship with your ABDL loved one. By recognizing the need for a safe space, practicing active listening, respecting boundaries, cultivating empathy and understanding, and seeking professional help when needed, you can establish an environment where open communication can thrive. Remember, acceptance and empathy are key in fostering a positive environment that supports your loved one's ABDL journey.

Active Listening and Empathy Techniques

In this subchapter, we will explore the essential skills of active listening and empathy techniques that can help family members navigate the complexities of ABDL boundaries and foster a healthy and respectful relationship with their loved ones.

Active listening is a fundamental skill that involves fully engaging with and understanding the other person's thoughts, feelings, and needs. When it comes to ABDL boundaries, active listening becomes even more critical as it allows non-ABDL family members to gain insight into their loved one's unique identity and experiences.

One of the key aspects of active listening is giving your undivided attention to the person speaking. Set aside distractions and make a conscious effort to focus on what they are saying. Maintain eye contact, nod, and use verbal cues to show that you are fully present and genuinely interested in their perspective.

Empathy is another vital skill that enables non-ABDL family members to understand and relate to their loved one's ABDL identity. It involves putting yourself in their shoes, trying to imagine how they feel and why they engage in this lifestyle. By practicing empathy, you can foster a safe and non-judgmental environment where open communication can thrive.

To demonstrate empathy, it is important to validate their feelings and experiences. Acknowledge their emotions and let them know that you are there to support them. Avoid making assumptions or passing judgments, as these can hinder open dialogue and create a barrier between you and your loved one.

Active listening and empathy techniques are not about agreeing with everything your loved one says or does. Rather, they are about showing respect, understanding, and a willingness to learn and grow together. By actively listening and practicing empathy, you can bridge the gap between your experiences and theirs, fostering a deeper connection and building a foundation of trust.

In this subchapter, we will provide practical strategies for active listening and empathy. We will explore techniques such as reflective listening, asking open-ended questions, and using non-verbal communication effectively. By incorporating these techniques into your interactions with your ABDL loved one, you can establish a positive and supportive environment where their boundaries are respected, and their identity is accepted.

Remember, navigating ABDL boundaries requires patience, compassion, and a genuine desire to understand. By actively listening and practicing empathy, you can strengthen your relationship with your loved one and create a space where they feel valued and accepted for who they are.

Setting Boundaries for Discussing ABDL Preferences

When it comes to discussing ABDL (Adult Baby/Diaper Lover) preferences with your loved ones, it is crucial to establish clear boundaries to ensure healthy and respectful communication. This subchapter aims to guide family members in navigating these boundaries and fostering open dialogue with their ABDL loved ones.

First and foremost, it is essential to remember that discussing ABDL preferences should always be approached with sensitivity and respect. Understand that your loved one's ABDL identity is a significant part of who they are, and it is crucial to create an environment that encourages open communication without judgment.

To establish boundaries, start by having an open and honest conversation with your loved one about their comfort levels. Ask them what topics they are willing to discuss and what they would prefer to keep private. Respect their boundaries and ensure that any information shared remains confidential.

In addition to respecting your loved one's boundaries, it is also important to set your own limits. Determine what you are comfortable discussing and what topics may make you uncomfortable. Communicate these boundaries to your loved one in a gentle and non-judgmental manner, emphasizing that your intent is to maintain a healthy and respectful relationship.

Remember that empathy plays a crucial role in understanding your loved one's ABDL preferences. Try to put yourself in their shoes and imagine what it must feel like to live with this aspect of their identity. This empathy will help you approach discussions with compassion and understanding, fostering a positive environment for both parties.

Furthermore, it is important to educate yourself about ABDL preferences and the broader ABDL community. Reading books, articles, or joining support groups can provide valuable insights and help dispel any misconceptions or stereotypes you may have. This knowledge will allow you to engage in informed conversations and offer support to your loved one.

Lastly, be patient with yourself and your loved one as you navigate these boundaries. Building a healthy and respectful relationship takes time and effort. Remember that open communication and understanding are key to maintaining a strong bond with your ABDL loved one.

In conclusion, setting boundaries for discussing ABDL preferences is crucial for maintaining a healthy and respectful relationship with your loved one. By respecting their boundaries, setting your own limits, practicing empathy, educating yourself, and fostering open communication, you can create a positive environment where discussions about ABDL preferences can take place with love and understanding.

Understanding Consent and Negotiating Boundaries in ABDL Play

In any relationship, understanding and respecting boundaries is crucial to maintaining a healthy and respectful dynamic. When it comes to the world of Adult Baby Diaper Lover (ABDL) play, it is even more important to navigate consent and negotiate boundaries effectively. This subchapter aims to provide family members with a comprehensive understanding of consent and the tools to establish open communication, ensuring a healthy and respectful relationship with their ABDL loved one.

Consent is the foundation of any healthy relationship, and it becomes even more important in the context of ABDL play. It is essential for family members to understand that ABDL play is a consensual and adult activity, and it is not inherently linked to pedophilia or any form of abuse. By educating ourselves and dispelling any misconceptions, we can foster a more accepting environment for our loved ones.

To navigate consent effectively, open communication is key. Family members should initiate a conversation with their ABDL loved one, expressing their willingness to listen and understand their desires and boundaries. Creating a safe space for open dialogue will allow both parties to express their needs, concerns, and limits. It is important to approach these discussions with empathy, understanding, and an open mind, avoiding judgment or criticism. This will help build trust and strengthen the bond between family members.

Negotiating boundaries in ABDL play is a collaborative process. Both parties should actively participate in establishing clear and mutually agreed-upon limits. It is crucial to remember that boundaries may evolve over time, and ongoing communication is essential to ensure that everyone involved feels comfortable and respected. Family members should be willing to adapt and accommodate their loved one's desires within their own personal comfort levels.

In addition to setting boundaries, it is equally important to discuss consent during ABDL play. Both parties should have a clear understanding of what is allowed and what is not. Establishing a safe word or signal can be helpful in communicating discomfort or the need to pause or stop the activity. This ensures that consent is ongoing and can be withdrawn at any time.

By understanding consent and negotiating boundaries effectively, family members can foster a healthy and respectful relationship with their ABDL loved one. Open communication, empathy, and a willingness to listen and understand are crucial in creating an environment that supports ABDL acceptance and the overall well-being of everyone involved.

Establishing Boundaries for Role Play Scenarios

Role play scenarios are a common aspect of the ABDL (Adult Baby Diaper Lover) lifestyle. For those who are unfamiliar with this lifestyle, it involves individuals who enjoy wearing diapers, regressing to a childlike state, and engaging in ageplay activities. While it may seem unusual or even uncomfortable for family members, it is important to approach this topic with an open mind and a willingness to understand.

In order to ensure a healthy and respectful relationship with your ABDL loved one, it is crucial to establish clear and consensual boundaries when it comes to role play scenarios. Here are some tips to help you navigate this sensitive topic:

1. Open Communication: The foundation of any healthy relationship is open communication. Talk to your loved one about their desires, interests, and limits when it comes to role play scenarios. Encourage them to express their feelings and concerns, and listen without judgment. This will create a safe space for them to share their needs and expectations.

2. Consent is Key: Consent is crucial in any role play scenario, and it is important to establish boundaries that both parties are comfortable with. Discuss what is off-limits and what is acceptable during role play sessions. Remember, consent can be withdrawn at any time, and it is essential to respect your loved one's boundaries.

3. Establish Safe Words: Safe words are a vital tool in role play scenarios. They allow the participants to communicate their comfort level during a scene. Encourage your loved one to choose a safe word that they feel comfortable using. This will ensure that they have an effective way to communicate if they want to pause or stop the role play.

4. Privacy and Discretion: ABDL role play scenarios are often considered intimate and personal. It is crucial to respect your loved one's privacy and keep their activities confidential. Avoid sharing their personal information or discussing their lifestyle with others without their consent.

5. Emotional Support: Understanding and accepting your loved one's ABDL identity can be challenging. However, offering emotional support is crucial for maintaining a healthy relationship. Be empathetic, ask questions, and educate yourself about the ABDL community. This will help you foster a positive environment where your loved one feels understood and accepted.

Remember, establishing boundaries for role play scenarios is a collaborative effort between you and your ABDL loved one. By approaching this topic with empathy, open-mindedness, and respect, you can build a stronger and more fulfilling relationship based on trust and understanding.

Creating a Safe Word System

In any relationship, communication is key. This is especially true when it comes to navigating ABDL boundaries with your loved ones. Establishing a safe word system can be an effective way to ensure open communication and maintain a healthy and respectful relationship with your ABDL family member. This subchapter will guide you on how to create a safe word system that works for both parties involved.

First and foremost, it is important to understand the purpose of a safe word. A safe word is a pre-agreed word or phrase that signals a need to pause, stop, or change the current situation. It is a tool to ensure that both parties feel safe, respected, and comfortable in any given situation.

When establishing a safe word system, it is crucial to involve your ABDL loved one in the process. Sit down together and have an open and honest conversation about the need for a safe word and what it means to both of you. This will help foster trust, understanding, and empathy.

Choose a safe word that is easy to remember and unrelated to any other words that may be commonly used in your everyday conversations. It should be something that is distinct and can be easily recognized in the heat of the moment. Remember, the purpose of a safe word is to immediately communicate a need for a change in the situation.

Once you have agreed upon a safe word, be consistent in its usage. Encourage your ABDL loved one to use the safe word whenever they feel uncomfortable, overwhelmed, or simply need a break. Similarly, as a family member, it is important for you to respect the safe word and respond accordingly. When the safe word is used, take a step back, evaluate the situation, and communicate openly about any concerns or needs.

Lastly, remember that the safe word system is not meant to be a way to control or manipulate your ABDL loved one. It is a tool to foster a healthy and respectful relationship built on trust, understanding, and open communication. It is important to regularly check in with your loved one to ensure that the safe word system is working effectively and to address any concerns or adjustments that may be needed.

By creating a safe word system, you are taking a proactive approach to navigate ABDL boundaries and establish a positive environment for both you and your ABDL loved one. It is a tangible way to show empathy, understanding, and support in their journey of self-acceptance and identity.

Communicating Comfort Levels and Limits

One of the most crucial aspects of maintaining a healthy and respectful relationship with your ABDL (Adult Baby/Diaper Lover) loved one is establishing open communication about comfort levels and limits. Both parties need to feel comfortable expressing their needs, boundaries, and expectations to ensure a fulfilling and supportive dynamic. This subchapter aims to guide family members in navigating these sensitive conversations, fostering understanding, empathy, and acceptance.

Understanding the ABDL Identity:

Before engaging in conversations about comfort levels and limits, it is essential to gain a comprehensive understanding of the ABDL identity. This involves educating yourself about the ABDL community, their motivations, and the psychological and emotional aspects involved. By familiarizing yourself with the subject matter, you will be better equipped to approach communication with an open mind and empathetic attitude.

Creating a Safe Space for Open Communication:

Establishing a safe and non-judgmental space for communication is vital. Encourage your loved one to express their desires, concerns, and boundaries without fear of ridicule or rejection. Active listening is key; allow them to speak without interruption and validate their feelings. Remember, this is an opportunity to deepen your understanding and strengthen your connection.

Setting Personal Boundaries:

As a family member, it is crucial to establish your own boundaries and comfort levels. Communicate these boundaries to your loved one in a calm and respectful manner. Be clear about your limitations, what you are comfortable participating in, and any concerns you may have. Transparency is essential to avoid misunderstandings and build trust.

Negotiating Compromises:

Once both parties have expressed their comfort levels and limits, it is necessary to find common ground. Negotiating compromises allows for a balanced relationship where both individuals' needs are met. Encourage open and honest discussions about which activities can be shared, modified, or avoided altogether. Remember that compromise is a two-way street, and finding a middle ground is crucial.

Continual Communication and Reevaluation:

Comfort levels and limits can evolve over time. It is vital to maintain ongoing communication to stay attuned to any changes or new boundaries. Encourage your loved one to express themselves freely and be receptive to their needs. Regularly reevaluate the dynamics of your relationship, ensuring that it remains healthy, respectful, and fulfilling for both parties.

By openly communicating comfort levels and limits, you can foster a positive environment where both you and your ABDL loved one feel supported and understood. Through empathy, understanding, and continual dialogue, you can navigate the complexities of ABDL boundaries and build a stronger, more resilient relationship.

Respecting Privacy and Confidentiality in ABDL Relationships

In any relationship, trust and respect for privacy are crucial. This is especially true when it comes to ABDL (Adult Baby/Diaper Lover) relationships. As family members of ABDL individuals, it is essential for you to understand and uphold the principles of privacy and confidentiality. By doing so, you can foster a healthy and respectful environment for your loved one.

Respecting privacy means recognizing and valuing an individual's right to keep certain aspects of their life private. In the context of ABDL relationships, this can include their choice to explore their ABDL identity and engage in ABDL activities. It is important to remember that these preferences are personal and may have a significant emotional significance for your loved one.

Confidentiality goes hand in hand with privacy. It involves keeping sensitive information shared by your ABDL loved one private and not discussing it with others without their explicit consent. This includes their ABDL identity, activities, and any other personal information they choose to disclose to you. Respecting confidentiality builds trust and demonstrates your commitment to their emotional well-being.

To navigate privacy and confidentiality boundaries effectively, open communication is key. Encourage your loved one to express their needs and boundaries, and listen attentively without judgment. Create a safe space where they can freely discuss their ABDL identity and experiences without fear of stigma or ridicule. By actively listening and showing empathy, you can foster a positive and accepting environment.

It is critical to emphasize that respecting privacy and confidentiality does not mean turning a blind eye to potential risks or harm. If you have genuine concerns about their well-being, it is essential to approach the situation with care and empathy. Seek their permission before discussing the matter with professionals or seeking guidance from support groups. Remember, your intention should always be to support and protect your loved one, while still respecting their privacy.

Lastly, it is important to educate yourself about ABDL identities and communities. By understanding the motivations, emotions, and experiences associated with ABDL, you can better empathize with your loved one's journey. This knowledge will help you foster a more accepting and supportive relationship, ultimately strengthening the bond between you.

In conclusion, respecting privacy and confidentiality is crucial in ABDL relationships. By upholding these principles, fostering open communication, and educating yourself, you can create a healthy and respectful environment for your ABDL loved one. Remember, your support and acceptance can make a significant difference in their overall happiness and well-being.

Discussing Social Media and Online Presence Boundaries

In today's digital age, social media has become an integral part of our lives. It allows us to connect with friends, share our experiences, and express ourselves freely. However, when it comes to ABDL (Adult Baby/Diaper Lover) individuals, navigating social media and online presence boundaries can be a sensitive topic.

As family members of ABDL individuals, it is essential for us to understand and respect their boundaries in the online realm. This subchapter aims to provide guidance on how to approach this topic and establish open communication to ensure a healthy and respectful relationship with our ABDL loved ones.

First and foremost, it is crucial to have an open and non-judgmental conversation with our loved ones about their online presence. Ask them how they feel about sharing their ABDL identity on social media platforms and whether they are comfortable with it. Respect their decision if they choose to keep it private or share it selectively.

It is equally important to educate ourselves about the potential risks and challenges that ABDL individuals may face online. Discuss the importance of maintaining privacy and the potential consequences of sharing personal information openly. Encourage them to be cautious about accepting friend requests or engaging in conversations with strangers online.

When it comes to our own presence on social media, we must be mindful of our loved one's comfort level. Avoid sharing or posting anything that may inadvertently reveal their ABDL identity without their consent. Respect their right to privacy and ensure that our own online activities do not compromise their well-being or cause them distress.

Additionally, fostering a positive and accepting environment offline can greatly impact our loved one's online experiences. By creating an atmosphere of understanding, empathy, and acceptance within the family, we can provide them with the confidence and support they need to navigate their online presence.

In conclusion, discussing social media and online presence boundaries with our ABDL loved ones is a crucial aspect of maintaining a healthy and respectful relationship. By having open and non-judgmental conversations, educating ourselves about potential risks, and fostering a positive environment, we can navigate this aspect of their lives together. Remember, it is essential to respect their boundaries and privacy, both online and offline, to ensure their well-being and happiness.

Addressing Concerns about Privacy with Friends and Family Members

Privacy is a fundamental aspect of everyone's life, and it becomes even more crucial when dealing with sensitive topics such as ABDL (Adult Baby/Diaper

Lover) boundaries. As a family member of an ABDL individual, it is essential to address concerns about privacy to ensure a healthy and respectful relationship with your loved one. This subchapter aims to provide guidance on navigating privacy concerns with friends and family members while supporting your ABDL loved one.

First and foremost, it is crucial to respect your loved one's privacy and confidentiality. Just like any other aspect of their life, their ABDL identity should be kept private unless they explicitly express their desire to share it. It is not your place to disclose their personal information without their consent, and doing so may breach their trust.

Open communication is key when addressing concerns about privacy. Initiate a conversation with your loved one to understand their boundaries and preferences regarding privacy. Respect their wishes and ask for their guidance on how to handle situations that may arise with friends and family members who may not be aware or accepting of their ABDL identity.

Educate your friends and family members about ABDL boundaries while emphasizing the importance of privacy. Help them understand that it is not their right to disclose or discuss your loved one's ABDL identity without permission. Encourage empathy and understanding, emphasizing the need to create a safe and non-judgmental environment for your loved one.

Establishing clear boundaries is essential for maintaining privacy. Encourage your loved one to communicate their boundaries to friends and family members themselves, if they feel comfortable doing so. This will empower them to take control of their privacy and ensure that their wishes are respected.

Finally, remember that acceptance and support are vital for your loved one's well-being. Embrace their ABDL identity with empathy and understanding, and encourage others to do the same. By fostering a positive environment that respects privacy, you can strengthen your relationship with your loved one and help them navigate their ABDL journey with confidence.

In conclusion, addressing concerns about privacy with friends and family members is crucial for establishing a healthy and respectful relationship with your ABDL loved one. By respecting their privacy, promoting open communication, educating others, establishing clear boundaries, and fostering acceptance, you can create a safe and supportive environment that allows your loved one to embrace their ABDL identity with confidence.

Handling Situations Involving Disclosure of ABDL Identity

Introduction:
When a family member discloses their ABDL (Adult Baby Diaper Lover) identity, it can be a challenging and unfamiliar situation for non-ABDL family members. This subchapter aims to provide guidance on how to handle these situations with empathy, understanding, and respect. By establishing open communication and setting boundaries, family members can create a healthy and supportive environment for their ABDL loved one.

1. Validate their feelings:
Upon disclosure, it is crucial to acknowledge and validate the emotions your loved one may be experiencing. Understand that discovering one's ABDL identity can be a vulnerable process, and they may have fears of judgment or rejection. Assure them that you love and accept them unconditionally, emphasizing that you are there to support them.

2. Educate yourself:
Take the time to educate yourself about ABDL identity. Familiarize yourself with the terminology, community, and reasons why individuals engage in ABDL activities. This knowledge will help you better understand their experiences and foster open communication.

3. Communicate openly:
Encourage open and honest conversations about their ABDL identity. Listen attentively without judgment, allowing them to share their thoughts, feelings,

and experiences. This communication will help build trust and create a safe space where they can express themselves freely.

4. Establish boundaries:
Work together to establish boundaries that respect both your loved one's ABDL identity and your own comfort levels. Discuss topics such as privacy, disclosure to others, and appropriate behavior within the family setting. By setting clear boundaries, you can ensure a respectful and healthy relationship for all involved.

5. Seek support:
Reach out to support groups or professionals who specialize in ABDL identity. They can offer guidance, resources, and a sense of community for both non-ABDL family members and ABDL individuals. This support system can provide valuable insights and help navigate any challenges that may arise.

Conclusion:
Handling situations involving the disclosure of an ABDL identity requires open-mindedness, empathy, and effective communication. By validating their feelings, educating yourself, establishing boundaries, and seeking support, you can foster a healthy and respectful relationship with your ABDL loved one. Remember, acceptance and understanding are the pillars of creating a positive environment for all family members involved.

Chapter 3: Building a Supportive Environment

Overcoming Negative Reactions and Stereotypes

Introduction:

In this subchapter, we will explore the importance of overcoming negative reactions and stereotypes when it comes to understanding and supporting your ABDL loved one. We understand that it can be challenging and unfamiliar territory for non-ABDL family members. However, by fostering open communication, empathy, and a positive environment, you can establish a healthy and respectful relationship with your ABDL family member.

Challenging Negative Reactions:

When discovering your loved one's ABDL identity, it is essential to approach the situation with an open mind. Negative reactions such as shock, confusion, or fear are common, but it is crucial to address and challenge these reactions. Instead of allowing stereotypes and misconceptions to dominate your thoughts, take the time to educate yourself about the ABDL community. By learning about the complexities and diversity within this community, you can better understand your loved one's perspective and experiences.

Empathy and Understanding:

Empathy is key to fostering a positive environment for your ABDL family member. Put yourself in their shoes and try to understand their desires and needs. Remember that being ABDL is a part of their identity, and it is crucial to accept and respect them for who they are. By showing empathy and understanding, you can create a safe space for open communication and help them feel validated and accepted.

Open Communication:

Establishing open and honest communication is vital in any relationship, and it is no different when it comes to dealing with ABDL boundaries. Encourage your loved one to express their needs, fears, and concerns openly. Create a judgment-free zone where they feel comfortable sharing their experiences and emotions. By actively listening and providing support, you can build trust and strengthen your bond.

Fostering a Positive Environment:

Creating a positive environment is crucial for your loved one's well-being. Ensure that your interactions are respectful, non-judgmental, and inclusive. Avoid making derogatory comments or jokes that may perpetuate negative stereotypes. Instead, focus on fostering an atmosphere of acceptance, love, and understanding.

Conclusion:

Overcoming negative reactions and stereotypes is a journey that requires open-mindedness, empathy, and a commitment to understanding. By challenging misconceptions, fostering open communication, and creating a positive environment, you can establish a healthy and respectful relationship with your ABDL loved one. Remember, your support and acceptance are crucial in helping them feel validated and loved as they navigate their ABDL identity.

Educating Family Members about ABDL

Navigating ABDL Boundaries: A Guide for Family Members

Chapter 3: Educating Family Members about ABDL

Introduction:
This chapter is designed to provide non-ABDL family members with a

comprehensive understanding of Adult Baby/Diaper Lover (ABDL) identities and practices. By educating yourself about ABDL, you can create a safe, loving, and respectful environment for your ABDL loved one. This chapter will address two crucial aspects: ABDL Boundaries and ABDL Acceptance.

ABDL Boundaries:
Understanding boundaries is crucial when navigating the ABDL lifestyle. It is essential to respect your loved one's boundaries while establishing open lines of communication. This section focuses on helping non-ABDL family members navigate these boundaries effectively.

1. Communication: Learn effective communication strategies to discuss ABDL preferences and boundaries. We provide practical tips on initiating conversations, active listening, and expressing concerns without judgment.

2. Consent: Explore the importance of consent in ABDL relationships. Understand how to create a comfortable space where consent is freely given and respected.

3. Privacy and Confidentiality: Discover the significance of privacy and confidentiality in the ABDL community. Learn how to respect your loved one's need for privacy and ensure that their personal information remains confidential.

ABDL Acceptance:
Acceptance is crucial in fostering a positive environment for your ABDL loved one. This section aims to help non-ABDL family members struggling with acceptance by providing guidance, empathy, and understanding.

1. Empathy and Understanding: Learn to empathize with your loved one's ABDL identity and understand the emotional complexities associated with it. Gain insights into the psychological and emotional aspects of ABDL experiences.

2. Breaking Taboos: Explore the societal taboos surrounding ABDL and how they impact your loved one's self-esteem and mental well-being. Discover ways to challenge these taboos and promote acceptance.

3. Fostering a Positive Environment: Understand how to create a positive and accepting environment for your loved one. We provide practical tips on using inclusive language, supporting their interests, and engaging in activities that promote their self-expression.

Conclusion:

By educating yourself about ABDL and understanding the boundaries and needs of your loved one, you can build a healthy, respectful, and accepting relationship. This chapter aims to equip you with the knowledge and tools needed to navigate the ABDL world and ensure your loved one feels loved and supported. Remember, your understanding and acceptance can make a significant difference in their overall well-being.

Addressing Common Concerns and Fears

Introduction:

As a family member, it is natural to have concerns and fears when confronted with unfamiliar territory. Discovering that your loved one is an ABDL (Adult Baby/Diaper Lover) can be a surprising and potentially challenging revelation. In this subchapter, we will address some common concerns and fears that family members may have when navigating ABDL boundaries. By understanding these concerns and fears, we can foster open communication, acceptance, empathy, and ultimately establish a healthy and respectful relationship with our ABDL loved ones.

1. Respecting Boundaries:

One common concern is how to respect the boundaries of our ABDL loved ones. It is important to remember that boundaries are unique to each individual, and what might be comfortable for one person may not be for another. Openly discussing boundaries and consent is crucial to ensure that both parties feel respected and understood.

2. Normalizing ABDL Identity:
Accepting that your loved one identifies as an ABDL may be difficult, as it challenges societal norms and expectations. It is essential to recognize that ABDL identity is a valid part of their identity and not a reflection of their character or morality. By educating ourselves about ABDL and seeking resources, we can better understand their experiences and struggles, fostering empathy and acceptance.

3. Communication and Support:
Open and honest communication is key in any relationship, including those involving ABDL identity. Encouraging your loved one to express their needs, desires, and concerns openly creates a safe space for dialogue. Active listening, non-judgmental attitudes, and unconditional support are essential in building trust and maintaining a healthy relationship.

4. Fostering a Positive Environment:
Creating a positive environment for your ABDL loved one is crucial for their well-being. This includes refraining from stigmatizing or shaming language, treating them with respect, and promoting inclusivity within the family. By fostering a safe and non-judgmental space, you can help your loved one feel accepted and understood.

Conclusion:
Navigating ABDL boundaries and accepting your loved one's identity may initially seem challenging. However, by addressing common concerns and fears, we can establish open communication, empathy, and understanding. It is important to remember that love and support are the foundations of any healthy relationship. By embracing these principles, we can build a strong and respectful connection with our ABDL loved ones, ultimately fostering a positive environment for everyone involved.

Encouraging Acceptance and Understanding

In this subchapter, we will delve into the essential aspects of encouraging acceptance and understanding within the context of an ABDL (Adult

Baby/Diaper Lover) identity. As a family member, it is crucial to establish open communication and maintain a healthy and respectful relationship with your ABDL loved one. By doing so, you can support them in their journey towards self-acceptance and foster a positive environment for everyone involved.

Understanding ABDL Boundaries:
When it comes to ABDL boundaries, it is vital to recognize that each individual has their own unique preferences and comfort levels. By acknowledging and respecting these boundaries, you can build trust and strengthen your relationship with your ABDL loved one. Communicate openly with them, asking questions to gain a better understanding of their needs, desires, and limitations. Remember, ABDL activities are consensual and should never be forced upon anyone.

Establishing Open Communication:
Creating a safe space for open communication is key to maintaining a healthy relationship with your ABDL loved one. Encourage them to share their feelings, thoughts, and experiences without fear of judgment or criticism. Actively listen to their stories, concerns, and desires, validating their emotions and experiences. By promoting open dialogue, you can develop a deeper understanding of their ABDL identity and create a stronger bond.

Empathy and Understanding:
It is natural for non-ABDL family members to struggle with accepting their loved one's ABDL identity. However, fostering empathy and understanding can help bridge the gap. Educate yourself about ABDL through resources, forums, or support groups. This knowledge will enable you to approach the topic with compassion and empathy. Remember, your loved one's ABDL identity does not define their entire being; they are still the same person you've always known and loved.

Fostering a Positive Environment:
Creating a positive environment is essential for the well-being of both you and your ABDL loved one. Celebrate their identity and encourage them to express

themselves freely within the agreed-upon boundaries. Avoid negative remarks or jokes that may belittle or shame them. Instead, focus on their strengths, talents, and other aspects of their life that go beyond their ABDL identity. By doing so, you can help your loved one feel accepted and loved unconditionally.

Remember, accepting and understanding your ABDL loved one may take time and effort. Be patient and open-minded, and recognize that this journey is unique to each family. By navigating boundaries, establishing open communication, and fostering a positive environment, you can forge a stronger connection with your ABDL loved one and create a supportive and loving family dynamic.

Fostering Positive Communication with Other Family Members

When it comes to navigating the world of ABDL boundaries and acceptance, fostering positive communication with other family members is crucial. Open and honest dialogue is the key to building a healthy and respectful relationship with your ABDL loved one. In this subchapter, we will explore effective strategies for improving communication within the family unit.

1. Active Listening: Listening is the foundation of effective communication. Make a conscious effort to give your full attention when your loved one is speaking. Show empathy, understanding, and validate their feelings. Avoid interrupting or dismissing their thoughts, as this can create a barrier to open communication.

2. Respect Boundaries: It is essential to respect your loved one's ABDL boundaries. Understand that everyone has their unique comfort levels and preferences. Never force conversations or invade their privacy. Instead, create a safe space where they feel comfortable discussing their needs and boundaries when they are ready.

3. Educate Yourself: To foster positive communication, educate yourself about ABDL identities and experiences. Learn about the psychological and emotional aspects of ABDL practice. This knowledge will help you approach conversations with sensitivity and understanding, enhancing your ability to connect with your loved one.

4. Non-Judgmental Attitude: Adopt a non-judgmental attitude towards your loved one's ABDL identity. Avoid making assumptions or passing judgment. Acceptance is key to creating an environment where open communication can flourish. Remember, your loved one's ABDL identity does not define their worth as a person.

5. Express Your Concerns: If you have concerns about your loved one's ABDL practice, express them in a calm and non-confrontational manner. Use "I" statements, focusing on your feelings rather than criticizing their actions. Remember, your goal is to foster understanding and empathy, not to change their identity.

6. Seek Professional Help: If you find it challenging to navigate ABDL boundaries or acceptance within your family, consider seeking professional help. Therapists specializing in ABDL issues can provide guidance and support for both you and your loved one. They can help facilitate healthy communication and address any underlying concerns.

Remember, fostering positive communication is an ongoing process that requires patience, understanding, and empathy. By following these strategies, you can create a safe and nurturing environment that strengthens your relationship with your ABDL loved one.

Tools for Discussing ABDL with Children and Teenagers

Introduction:
Discussing ABDL (Adult Baby/Diaper Lover) with children and teenagers can

be challenging for family members who may be unfamiliar with this aspect of their loved one's identity. However, open communication and understanding are essential to ensure a healthy and respectful relationship. This subchapter aims to provide family members with practical tools and guidance on discussing ABDL with children and teenagers, promoting acceptance, empathy, and a positive environment.

1. Age-appropriate language:
When discussing ABDL with children and teenagers, it is crucial to use age-appropriate language. Avoid using complex or technical terms and opt for simple, understandable explanations. Use examples and analogies to help them grasp the concept without overwhelming them.

2. Active listening:
Listening is a fundamental tool for effective communication. Give your children or teenagers the space to express their thoughts, feelings, and concerns about ABDL. Validate their emotions and actively listen without judgment or interruption. This will foster trust and create an environment where they feel safe to share their thoughts openly.

3. Educate yourself:
Before discussing ABDL with your children or teenagers, take the time to educate yourself about this identity. Understand the motivations, desires, and emotional needs behind ABDL. This will enable you to answer their questions, address any misconceptions, and respond with empathy and understanding.

4. Normalize ABDL:
Normalize the ABDL identity by emphasizing that it is a part of who your loved one is. Explain that everyone has unique interests and preferences, and ABDL is just one facet of their personality. Encourage acceptance and emphasize that it is okay to be different.

5. Set boundaries:
Discussing boundaries is crucial for both the ABDL individual and their

family members. Talk openly about what is comfortable and respectful for everyone involved. Encourage open dialogue and ensure that your children or teenagers feel comfortable expressing their boundaries and concerns.

6. Seek professional help if needed:
If discussing ABDL becomes challenging or if you feel ill-equipped to handle the conversation, consider seeking professional help. A therapist or counselor experienced in working with families can provide guidance, support, and facilitate productive conversations.

Conclusion:
Open communication and understanding are vital when discussing ABDL with children and teenagers. By using age-appropriate language, actively listening, educating yourself, normalizing ABDL, setting boundaries, and seeking professional help if needed, family members can navigate these discussions successfully. Remember, fostering acceptance, empathy, and a positive environment is key to maintaining a healthy and respectful relationship with your ABDL loved one.

Navigating ABDL Boundaries within Extended Family Relationships

Introduction:
In this subchapter, we will explore the delicate subject of navigating ABDL (Adult Baby/Diaper Lover) boundaries within extended family relationships. It is crucial for family members to understand and respect the needs and boundaries of their ABDL loved ones. By establishing open communication and fostering a healthy and respectful environment, we can strengthen our relationships and ensure a positive experience for everyone involved.

Understanding ABDL Boundaries:
To begin, it is essential for family members to educate themselves about the ABDL lifestyle. This understanding will help dispel any misconceptions or preconceived notions that may hinder open communication. By exploring the

motivations, desires, and challenges faced by ABDL individuals, we can develop empathy and gain a deeper understanding of their needs.

Respecting Boundaries:
Respect for boundaries is the cornerstone of any healthy relationship. When it comes to ABDL individuals, it is crucial to respect their privacy and personal space. This may involve refraining from discussing their ABDL interests with others without their consent or asking intrusive questions. By showing respect, we can foster an environment of trust and acceptance.

Establishing Open Communication:
Open and honest communication is key to navigating ABDL boundaries within extended family relationships. Encourage your loved one to express their needs and preferences, and be receptive and non-judgmental when they do. By actively listening and engaging in a dialogue, we can ensure that their boundaries are understood and respected.

Creating a Positive Environment:
Creating a positive environment for your ABDL loved one involves fostering acceptance, empathy, and understanding. Educate other family members about the ABDL lifestyle, providing resources and guidance to help them overcome any challenges they may face in accepting their loved one's identity. By promoting an atmosphere of support and understanding, we can strengthen family bonds and create a safe space for everyone involved.

Conclusion:
Navigating ABDL boundaries within extended family relationships requires empathy, open communication, and a commitment to respect. By understanding the needs and preferences of your loved one, respecting their boundaries, and fostering a positive environment, you can ensure a healthy and respectful relationship. Remember, acceptance and understanding are vital in creating a supportive space for your ABDL loved one and strengthening family ties.

Seeking Professional Support and Counseling for Difficult Situations

In the journey of navigating ABDL boundaries and fostering a healthy relationship with your ABDL loved one, there may be times when you encounter difficult situations that require professional support and counseling. It is important to recognize that seeking outside help is not a sign of weakness, but rather a proactive step towards understanding and growth.

Professional support can come in various forms, such as therapy, counseling, or support groups. These resources are designed to provide you with a safe space to express your concerns, fears, and questions, and to help you navigate the unique challenges that may arise in your relationship with your ABDL loved one.

Therapy or counseling sessions can offer a non-judgmental and confidential environment where you can freely explore your thoughts and emotions. A trained professional can help you understand your own reactions, biases, and limitations, as well as provide guidance on effective communication strategies and problem-solving techniques. They can also offer insights into the ABDL community and help you develop empathy and understanding towards your loved one's ABDL identity.

Support groups specifically tailored for family members of ABDL individuals can be incredibly beneficial. These groups create a sense of community and allow you to connect with others who may be going through similar experiences. Sharing your stories, listening to others, and exchanging advice can provide a valuable support network and a source of comfort during challenging times.

Remember that seeking professional support and counseling does not mean you are giving up or failing as a family member. Rather, it demonstrates your commitment to understanding, acceptance, and growth within your relationship. It shows that you are willing to put in the effort to foster a healthy and respectful environment for both yourself and your ABDL loved one.

As you embark on this journey, keep in mind that professional support is just one aspect of navigating ABDL boundaries. Open and honest communication, empathy, and a willingness to learn are equally important. By combining these elements, you can create a positive and accepting environment that will strengthen your relationship with your ABDL loved one and promote their overall well-being.

Seeking professional support and counseling is a courageous step towards personal and relational growth. Embrace the opportunity to learn and grow, and remember that you are not alone in this journey. With the right support system and resources, you can navigate the challenges and establish a healthy and respectful relationship with your ABDL loved one.

Creating a Supportive Network for ABDL Loved Ones

Introduction:
When a family member identifies as an Adult Baby/Diaper Lover (ABDL), it can be challenging for their loved ones to understand and support them. This subchapter aims to provide guidance for family members on how to create a supportive network for their ABDL loved ones. By establishing open communication, setting boundaries, and fostering an accepting environment, families can build healthy and respectful relationships with their ABDL family members.

1. Open Communication:
Effective communication is the foundation of any healthy relationship. Begin by initiating an open and non-judgmental dialogue with your ABDL loved one. Encourage them to express their feelings, desires, and concerns openly. Actively listen and validate their emotions, even if you don't fully understand their ABDL identity.

2. Understanding Boundaries:
Respecting each other's boundaries is crucial to maintaining a positive relationship. Discuss and establish boundaries together, ensuring that both parties feel comfortable and safe. Understand that each ABDL individual may have unique preferences and limits, and it's essential to respect these boundaries without judgment or ridicule.

3. Seeking Support:
Navigating the ABDL world can be overwhelming for non-ABDL family members. Reach out to support groups, therapists, or online communities specifically designed for families of ABDL individuals. These resources can provide valuable guidance, answer questions, and offer a safe space to share experiences and concerns.

4. Education and Empathy:
Educate yourself about the ABDL community and the reasons behind your loved one's identification. Foster empathy by trying to understand their needs, desires, and emotions. Recognize that their ABDL identity is a valid part of who they are and that acceptance and understanding are essential for their well-being.

5. Creating a Positive Environment:
To create a supportive network, it's crucial to foster a positive environment for your ABDL loved one. Avoid judgment, criticism, or shaming, as this can damage their self-esteem and strain your relationship. Encourage open-mindedness and acceptance within the family, promoting love, understanding, and support.

Conclusion:
Supporting an ABDL loved one requires open communication, understanding boundaries, seeking support, educating oneself, and creating a positive environment. By implementing these strategies, non-ABDL family members can navigate their loved one's ABDL identity with empathy and respect, fostering healthy and respectful relationships. Remember, acceptance and support are fundamental in building a strong and loving family bond.

Connecting with ABDL Communities and Support Groups

One of the most important steps in understanding and supporting your ABDL loved one is to connect with ABDL communities and support groups. These communities can provide valuable insights, advice, and guidance on navigating the boundaries and challenges that may arise in your relationship. By reaching out and connecting with others who have similar experiences, you can find comfort, understanding, and a sense of community.

ABDL communities and support groups offer a safe space for family members to share their stories, ask questions, and seek guidance from others who have been through similar situations. These groups often have online forums, chat rooms, and social media platforms where you can connect with others and learn from their experiences. By joining these communities, you can gain a greater understanding of the ABDL lifestyle, its complexities, and the challenges your loved one may face.

Through these connections, you can also learn about resources and strategies for setting boundaries and establishing open communication with your ABDL loved one. These communities often provide valuable advice on how to approach difficult conversations, address concerns, and maintain a healthy and respectful relationship. By engaging with others who have successfully navigated similar situations, you can gain confidence and tools to better support your loved one.

In addition to online communities, there are often local support groups that meet in person. These groups provide a safe and supportive environment for family members to discuss their experiences, share advice, and learn from experts in the field. Attending these meetings can be an opportunity to connect with others who understand your journey and provide a network of support.

Connecting with ABDL communities and support groups is also beneficial for those struggling with accepting their loved one's ABDL identity. These communities can offer guidance on empathy, understanding, and fostering a positive environment. By hearing stories of acceptance and learning from others who have overcome their own struggles, you can find hope and inspiration to embrace your loved one's identity fully.

In conclusion, connecting with ABDL communities and support groups is a crucial step in navigating boundaries and establishing open communication with your ABDL loved one. These communities provide a safe and understanding space where you can share your experiences, seek advice, and gain insights from others who have walked a similar path. By engaging with these communities, you can find comfort, support, and resources to better understand and support your loved one.

Finding Online Resources and Forums for ABDL Family Members

In today's digital age, the internet has become an invaluable tool for connecting individuals with similar interests and experiences. For family members of ABDL individuals, finding online resources and forums can be an essential step in understanding and supporting their loved one's ABDL identity. This subchapter aims to guide family members in navigating the vast online landscape to find reliable and helpful resources.

When it comes to finding online resources for ABDL family members, one of the first places to start is dedicated websites and forums. These platforms provide a safe and inclusive space for ABDL individuals and their loved ones to share experiences, ask questions, and seek advice. Some popular ABDL websites and forums include ABDLmatch, DailyDiapers, and ABDLforum. These platforms often have specific sections or threads dedicated to family members, where they can find support from others who have navigated similar situations.

In addition to dedicated ABDL websites and forums, social media can also be a valuable resource. Platforms such as Facebook, Reddit, and Tumblr have

communities and groups dedicated to ABDL individuals and their families.
These groups can provide a wealth of information, personal stories, and a
platform for open discussion. By joining these groups, family members can
connect with others who are going through similar experiences, share their
concerns, and gain insights into the ABDL community.

It is important to note that while online resources and forums can be incredibly
helpful, it is crucial to approach them with caution and critical thinking. Not
all information found online may be accurate or helpful, so it is essential to
verify the credibility of sources and rely on reputable websites and forums.

Ultimately, finding online resources and forums for ABDL family members
can provide a sense of community, support, and understanding. It allows
family members to connect with others who have walked a similar path, gain
insights into their loved one's ABDL identity, and establish open
communication channels. By utilizing these online platforms, family members
can foster a healthy and respectful relationship with their ABDL loved one,
ensuring a positive and accepting environment for everyone involved.

Engaging in Self-Care and Seeking Personal Support

Taking care of oneself is essential when navigating the boundaries of the
ABDL community as a family member. It is important to remember that
supporting your ABDL loved one does not mean neglecting your own needs.
Engaging in self-care and seeking personal support can help you maintain a
healthy and respectful relationship with your ABDL family member.

Self-care involves prioritizing your physical, emotional, and mental well-
being. It means carving out time for activities that bring you joy, relaxation,
and rejuvenation. Engaging in self-care can help manage stress and prevent
burnout, allowing you to be present and supportive for your ABDL loved one.

Here are some self-care strategies you can consider:

1. Find a support network: Connect with other family members who are navigating similar experiences. Joining online forums or support groups can provide a safe space to share your thoughts, concerns, and receive advice from individuals who understand your situation.

2. Set boundaries: Establishing clear boundaries is crucial for maintaining your own well-being. Communicate your needs openly and honestly with your ABDL family member. This will help create a balanced and respectful relationship.

3. Educate yourself: Take the time to learn more about the ABDL community, its practices, and the reasons behind it. Understanding your loved one's identity can foster empathy, compassion, and acceptance within your family.

4. Practice self-compassion: It is natural to experience a range of emotions when supporting your ABDL loved one. Practice self-compassion by acknowledging and accepting your feelings without judgment. Treat yourself with kindness and understanding during challenging moments.

5. Take breaks: Recognize when you need some time for yourself. Engage in activities that recharge you, such as hobbies, exercise, or spending time with friends and loved ones. Taking breaks can help you maintain your own emotional balance.

Remember, seeking personal support is not a sign of weakness. It is a proactive step towards maintaining your own well-being and fostering a healthy and respectful relationship with your ABDL loved one. By engaging in self-care and seeking support, you can navigate the boundaries of the ABDL community more effectively and establish open communication within your family.

Chapter 4: Embracing ABDL Identity

Understanding the Origins and Diversity of ABDL Identity

Introduction:

In this subchapter, we delve into the origins and diversity of the ABDL (Adult Baby Diaper Lover) identity. By exploring the roots of this unique lifestyle and understanding its diverse manifestations, we aim to provide family members with a comprehensive understanding of their loved one's ABDL identity. This knowledge will enable them to navigate boundaries, establish open communication, and foster a healthy and respectful relationship.

Origins of ABDL Identity:

The ABDL identity emerged from various sources, including psychological theories, childhood experiences, and personal preferences. Some individuals attribute their ABDL identity to childhood memories, where wearing diapers or engaging in age-regressive behaviors provided comfort and a sense of security. Others find solace in the idea of relinquishing adult responsibilities and embracing a childlike state. Additionally, some psychological theories suggest that the ABDL identity may stem from a desire to cope with stress or trauma.

Diversity within the ABDL Community:

It is crucial for family members to recognize the diversity within the ABDL community. ABDL individuals may have varying preferences and engage in different activities within the lifestyle. Some may focus solely on the wearing of diapers, while others may incorporate age-regressive activities, such as using baby items or engaging in role-playing scenarios. It is essential to approach each individual's preferences with empathy and understanding, acknowledging that their choices do not diminish their worth or character.

Navigating Boundaries:

Understanding and respecting boundaries are vital for maintaining a healthy relationship with an ABDL loved one. It is crucial to establish open communication channels where both parties can express their thoughts, concerns, and expectations. By actively listening and engaging in non-judgmental conversations, family members can create an environment of trust and acceptance. Setting clear boundaries together, based on mutual consent and respect, will help ensure that everyone's needs are met.

Fostering Acceptance:

For family members struggling with accepting their loved one's ABDL identity, empathy and understanding are key. Educating oneself about the ABDL community, its origins, and the experiences of ABDL individuals can foster acceptance and empathy. It is essential to distinguish between the ABDL identity and any preconceived notions or stereotypes, appreciating that this lifestyle is a valid and consensual choice. Creating a positive and supportive environment that encourages open dialogue and offers emotional support will help non-ABDL family members navigate their journey towards acceptance.

Conclusion:

Understanding the origins and diversity of the ABDL identity is crucial for family members striving to establish healthy and respectful relationships with their ABDL loved ones. By acknowledging the various sources and manifestations of the ABDL identity, family members can navigate boundaries, foster open communication, and create an environment of acceptance. This subchapter equips family members with the knowledge and empathy needed to ensure a positive and supportive relationship with their ABDL loved ones.

Challenging Stigma and Promoting Acceptance

In a world where diversity and acceptance are increasingly valued, it is essential for family members to challenge stigma and promote acceptance when it comes to their ABDL loved ones. This subchapter aims to provide practical guidance on how non-ABDL family members can navigate boundaries and establish open communication, fostering a healthy and respectful relationship with their ABDL family member.

Understanding ABDL Boundaries

To navigate ABDL boundaries effectively, it is crucial to educate oneself about this unique identity. ABDL stands for Adult Baby/Diaper Lover and refers to individuals who find comfort, enjoyment, or stress relief through age regression or wearing diapers. By learning about the ABDL community, its history, and the various aspects of this identity, family members can gain a deeper understanding of their loved one's needs and desires.

Open Communication and Boundaries

Open communication is the foundation of any healthy relationship. It is important for family members to establish a safe space where their ABDL loved one feels comfortable expressing their feelings, thoughts, and boundaries. Encouraging open dialogue about their ABDL identity can help foster trust and mutual understanding.

Respecting Boundaries

Respecting boundaries is crucial in maintaining a healthy and respectful relationship with an ABDL family member. Each individual's boundaries may vary, and it is essential to respect and honor them. This includes understanding their preferences regarding privacy, participating in ABDL activities, or discussing their identity openly. By doing so, family members can create an environment where their loved one feels accepted and valued.

Empathy and Understanding

Empathy and understanding play a significant role in accepting an ABDL family member's identity. It is important to recognize that being ABDL is not a choice but a fundamental aspect of their being. By putting oneself in their shoes, family members can develop a deeper sense of empathy and compassion, allowing for a more supportive and accepting environment.

Fostering a Positive Environment

Creating a positive environment is essential for the emotional well-being of both the ABDL individual and their family members. This includes avoiding judgmental attitudes, promoting open-mindedness, and celebrating the uniqueness of each family member. By fostering a positive environment, family members can help their loved one feel accepted, loved, and supported.

Conclusion

Challenging stigma and promoting acceptance is a journey that requires effort, empathy, and understanding. By navigating ABDL boundaries, establishing open communication, and fostering a positive environment, family members can create a space where their ABDL loved one feels accepted and valued. Embracing diversity and promoting acceptance is a powerful way to strengthen family bonds and ensure a healthy and respectful relationship with an ABDL family member.

Educating Friends and Family Members about ABDL Identity

Subchapter: Educating Friends and Family Members about ABDL Identity

Introduction:
Understanding the ABDL (Adult Baby/Diaper Lover) identity can be a complex process for family members who are not familiar with it. This subchapter aims to provide guidance to family members on how to educate themselves and others about the ABDL identity. By fostering open communication and creating a positive environment, family members can ensure a healthy and respectful relationship with their ABDL loved one.

1. The Importance of Education:
It is crucial for family members to educate themselves about the ABDL identity. By understanding the intricacies of this identity, they can provide better support and foster a more inclusive environment. Education helps dispel misconceptions, reduce stigma, and promote empathy within the family.

2. Open Communication:
Establishing open and honest communication is key in navigating ABDL boundaries. Encourage family members to have open conversations about the ABDL identity, allowing the ABDL individual to share their experiences, thoughts, and feelings. This can help bridge the gap in understanding and build trust.

3. Providing Resources:
Offering resources such as books, articles, and online communities can be beneficial for family members seeking a deeper understanding of the ABDL identity. These resources can provide valuable insights, personal stories, and expert advice to help family members navigate their loved one's ABDL journey.

4. Empathy and Understanding:
Encourage family members to practice empathy and understanding when interacting with their ABDL loved one. Remind them that the ABDL identity is a valid form of self-expression and should be respected. Help them understand that ABDL is not a fetish but rather a way for individuals to explore their inner child and find comfort.

5. Fostering a Positive Environment:
Creating a positive and accepting environment is vital for the emotional well-being of ABDL individuals. Family members should be encouraged to embrace their loved one's ABDL identity and avoid judgment or ridicule. By fostering an environment of acceptance, love, and support, family members can help their loved one feel comfortable and secure.

Conclusion:
Educating friends and family members about the ABDL identity is crucial for establishing healthy and respectful relationships. By promoting open communication, providing resources, practicing empathy, and fostering a positive environment, family members can support their ABDL loved ones on their journey of self-discovery and acceptance. Remember, understanding and acceptance are the foundations of a strong and loving family bond.

Encouraging Empathy and Open-Mindedness

In this subchapter, we will explore the importance of empathy and open-mindedness when it comes to navigating ABDL (Adult Baby/Diaper Lover) boundaries within the context of family relationships. It is crucial for family members to understand and respect their ABDL loved one's identity, while also fostering a healthy and respectful environment for open communication.

Empathy is the cornerstone of any successful relationship. It involves putting oneself in another person's shoes and genuinely trying to understand their perspective. When it comes to ABDL individuals, it is essential for family members to demonstrate empathy by acknowledging and accepting their loved one's identity. Remember, ABDL is a part of who they are, and it does not define their worth or character.

Open-mindedness goes hand in hand with empathy. It means being receptive to new ideas, experiences, and perspectives without judgment or prejudice. By embracing open-mindedness, family members can create a safe space where their ABDL loved one feels comfortable expressing their needs and desires. This will help establish open communication channels and foster a deeper understanding of each other's boundaries.

To encourage empathy and open-mindedness within your family, it is vital to educate yourself about ABDL. Learn about the community, its history, and the motivations behind it. This knowledge will allow you to approach conversations with your loved one from an informed perspective and avoid making assumptions or generalizations.

Practice active listening when engaging in discussions about ABDL boundaries. Give your loved one the space to express themselves without interruption or judgment. Reflect back their feelings and thoughts to show that you genuinely understand and empathize with their perspective. This will build trust and strengthen your relationship.

Creating a positive environment is crucial for supporting your ABDL loved one's identity. Avoid negative comments, jokes, or shaming. Instead, focus on fostering acceptance, understanding, and love. Encourage open dialogue, where both parties can discuss their concerns and boundaries openly.

Remember, acceptance takes time, and it is okay to have questions or concerns. Approach these conversations with curiosity and a genuine desire to learn and understand. By demonstrating empathy and open-mindedness, you can establish a healthy and respectful relationship with your ABDL loved one, built on trust, understanding, and love.

In the next subchapter, we will delve deeper into the challenges non-ABDL family members may face when accepting their loved one's ABDL identity. We will provide guidance on overcoming these challenges and offer strategies for fostering acceptance within the family unit.

Promoting Positive Media Representations of ABDL

In today's digital age, media plays a significant role in shaping public perceptions and attitudes towards various communities and identities. Unfortunately, the Adult Baby Diaper Lover (ABDL) community often faces negative stereotypes and misconceptions in the media. As family members, it is crucial to promote positive representations of ABDL individuals to foster understanding, acceptance, and respect within our relationships.

One of the most effective ways to challenge stereotypes is by actively seeking out and supporting media that portrays ABDL individuals in a respectful and non-exploitative manner. Encourage family members to explore different forms of media, such as books, movies, documentaries, and online platforms that provide accurate and empathetic representations of ABDL experiences. By doing so, we can educate ourselves and challenge preconceived notions that may hinder our ability to support our loved ones.

Another way to promote positive media representations is to engage in open and honest conversations about the media we consume. Discuss with family members the impact that negative portrayals can have on the ABDL community and the importance of seeking out more accurate and inclusive representations. Encourage critical thinking and media literacy skills, helping them to identify the difference between harmful stereotypes and genuine attempts to promote understanding.

Additionally, it is vital to support ABDL creators and artists who are working towards portraying the community in a positive light. By purchasing books, artwork, or other forms of media created by ABDL individuals themselves, we can contribute to a more diverse and authentic representation of the community. This not only supports ABDL individuals in their creative endeavors but also helps to amplify their voices and experiences.

Lastly, it is essential to highlight instances of positive media representations when they do occur. Share articles, videos, or any other media that accurately portrays ABDL individuals with your friends and family. By sharing these examples, we can challenge misconceptions and encourage others to be more open-minded and accepting.

Promoting positive media representations of ABDL individuals is crucial for creating a more inclusive and understanding society. By actively seeking out accurate and empathetic portrayals, engaging in open conversations, supporting ABDL creators, and highlighting positive media examples, we can help change the narrative surrounding ABDL and foster a more accepting environment for our loved ones.

Supporting ABDL Loved Ones in Exploring and Expressing Their Identity

Introduction:
Discovering that a family member identifies as an Adult Baby/Diaper Lover (ABDL) can be a challenging experience. However, it is important to remember that supporting our loved ones in exploring and expressing their identity is crucial for their well-being and for maintaining a healthy and respectful relationship. This subchapter aims to provide guidance and strategies for family members on how to navigate this journey with their ABDL loved one.

1. Open Communication:
Establishing open and honest communication is essential in supporting ABDL loved ones. Create a safe space where they feel comfortable sharing their desires, concerns, and experiences. Listen attentively and avoid judgment, as it is vital to foster trust and understanding.

2. Educate Yourself:

Take the initiative to learn more about the ABDL community. Familiarize yourself with the terminology, understanding that this is a valid and diverse identity. Educating yourself will help dispel myths and misconceptions, allowing you to approach the topic with empathy and understanding.

3. Respect Boundaries:

Respecting your loved one's boundaries is crucial. Understand that not all aspects of their ABDL identity may be shared or discussed openly. Allow them to determine what they are comfortable sharing with you and others. Boundaries are essential in maintaining a healthy relationship and promoting trust.

4. Seek Support:

Navigating this journey alone can be overwhelming. Seek support from other family members or friends who may have gone through a similar experience. Online communities and support groups can also provide valuable insight and guidance. Remember, you are not alone, and reaching out for support is a sign of strength.

5. Foster a Positive Environment:

Creating a positive and accepting environment is essential for your ABDL loved one's well-being. Avoid making negative comments or judgments about their identity. Instead, focus on fostering a supportive atmosphere that encourages self-expression and personal growth.

Conclusion:

Supporting ABDL loved ones in exploring and expressing their identity requires open communication, understanding, and respect for boundaries. By educating ourselves, seeking support, and fostering a positive environment, we can ensure a healthy and respectful relationship with our ABDL family member. Remember, acceptance and empathy are key in navigating this journey together.

Encouraging Self-Discovery and Self-Acceptance

In any family relationship, it is essential to foster an environment of self-discovery and self-acceptance. This is especially true when it comes to navigating the boundaries of an ABDL (Adult Baby/Diaper Lover) loved one. Understanding and supporting their journey towards self-discovery and self-acceptance can be a powerful way to build a healthy and respectful relationship.

1. Creating a Safe Space: It is crucial to establish a safe and non-judgmental space where your ABDL loved one feels comfortable exploring their identity. This means setting aside any preconceived notions or biases and truly listening to their experiences and feelings. Encouraging open and honest communication is the first step towards self-discovery.

2. Practicing Empathy and Understanding: It is important to approach your loved one's ABDL identity with empathy and understanding. Put yourself in their shoes and try to comprehend the emotions and desires they are experiencing. By doing so, you can foster a deeper connection and strengthen your relationship.

3. Educate Yourself: Take the initiative to educate yourself about ABDL culture, its history, and the experiences of those who identify as ABDL. This will enable you to have informed conversations and provide support based on a solid understanding of their needs and desires.

4. Encourage Self-Reflection: Encourage your loved one to engage in self-reflection and exploration of their ABDL identity. This might involve journaling, seeking therapy, or connecting with supportive communities. By actively engaging in this process, they can better understand themselves and their desires.

5. Offer Unconditional Acceptance: It is vital to offer your loved one unconditional acceptance throughout their journey. Let them know that you love and support them, regardless of their ABDL identity. This acceptance will create a safe and positive environment for their self-discovery and self-acceptance.

6. Seek Professional Help if Needed: If you find it challenging to navigate these boundaries or if your loved one is struggling with self-acceptance, consider seeking the guidance of a therapist or counselor who specializes in ABDL issues. They can provide valuable insights and strategies for fostering a healthy and supportive relationship.

Remember, encouraging self-discovery and self-acceptance is a lifelong process. It requires patience, understanding, and open communication. By actively engaging in this journey alongside your ABDL loved one, you can build a stronger and more meaningful relationship based on trust, empathy, and acceptance.

Providing Emotional Support during ABDL Exploration

One of the most important aspects of supporting your ABDL loved one during their exploration is providing emotional support. Understanding and empathizing with their journey is crucial in maintaining a healthy and respectful relationship. In this subchapter, we will discuss effective strategies for providing emotional support during ABDL exploration.

1. Open Communication: Establishing open communication channels is key to providing emotional support. Encourage your loved one to share their thoughts, feelings, and experiences without judgment. Create a safe space where they can freely express themselves and be heard.

2. Active Listening: Practice active listening by giving your full attention to your loved one when they are sharing their thoughts and experiences. Avoid

interrupting or offering unsolicited advice. Instead, show genuine interest and validate their emotions.

3. Empathy and Understanding: It is essential to cultivate empathy and understanding towards your ABDL loved one. Try to put yourself in their shoes and imagine what it must be like to navigate their identity. Validate their feelings and let them know that you are there to support them unconditionally.

4. Research and Educate Yourself: Take the initiative to educate yourself about ABDL identity. Learn about the various aspects, motivations, and challenges associated with ABDL exploration. This will not only help you better understand your loved one but also allow you to have informed conversations and provide them with the support they need.

5. Offer Reassurance: ABDL exploration can often be accompanied by feelings of shame, guilt, or fear of judgment. Offering reassurance and reminding your loved one that their identity is valid and accepted can go a long way in providing emotional support. Let them know that you love and accept them for who they are.

6. Create a Positive Environment: Foster a positive environment where your loved one feels comfortable and accepted. Avoid making derogatory or judgmental comments about ABDL identity. Encourage them to explore their interests and hobbies related to ABDL in a supportive manner.

7. Seek Professional Help if Needed: If you feel overwhelmed or unsure about how to provide adequate emotional support, do not hesitate to seek professional help. A therapist experienced in working with ABDL individuals and their families can provide guidance and help navigate any challenges you may face.

Remember, providing emotional support to your ABDL loved one is an ongoing process. Be patient, understanding, and willing to learn and grow together. By doing so, you can establish a strong, healthy, and respectful relationship with your loved one, fostering an environment of acceptance and understanding.

Assisting in Finding Accepting ABDL Communities and Partnerships

One of the most crucial aspects of supporting your ABDL loved one is helping them find accepting and understanding communities and partnerships. By doing so, you can play an instrumental role in fostering their sense of belonging and overall well-being. In this subchapter, we will discuss various strategies and resources that can assist you in this endeavor.

1. Online platforms and forums: The internet offers a wealth of online communities dedicated to ABDL individuals. These platforms provide a safe and inclusive space where your loved one can connect with like-minded individuals, share experiences, and seek advice. Encourage them to explore these platforms and ensure they understand the importance of online safety and privacy.

2. Support groups: Local support groups can be a valuable resource for both ABDL individuals and their families. These groups offer a safe and non-judgmental environment where your loved one can meet others who share similar experiences. Research local support groups in your area and consider attending meetings together to show your support and gain a better understanding of the community.

3. ABDL conventions and events: Attending ABDL conventions and events can be an empowering experience for your loved one. These gatherings offer an opportunity for them to meet like-minded individuals face-to-face, participate in workshops, and celebrate their identity openly. Help them research local events and accompany them if they feel comfortable.

4. Social media groups: Many ABDL individuals find support and acceptance through social media groups dedicated to the community. These groups allow

them to connect with individuals from all over the world, sharing stories, advice, and experiences. Encourage your loved one to explore these groups, but remind them to exercise caution and ensure they are joining reputable and safe communities.

5. Partner acceptance: Supporting your loved one in finding accepting partnerships can be immensely beneficial to their emotional well-being. Encourage open communication about their ABDL identity within their relationships and provide guidance on how to broach the topic with potential partners. Remind them that finding a partner who accepts and understands their ABDL identity is possible, but it may require patience and persistence.

Remember, your role as a family member is to be a supportive ally throughout your loved one's journey. By assisting them in finding accepting communities and partnerships, you are not only fostering their happiness but also contributing to a more inclusive and understanding society.

Chapter 5: Nurturing a Healthy and Respectful Relationship

Building Trust and Intimacy in ABDL Relationships

Trust and intimacy are crucial aspects of any relationship, including those involving ABDL (Adult Baby/Diaper Lover) individuals. As a family member of an ABDL loved one, it is essential to understand how to navigate these elements to ensure a healthy and respectful relationship. This chapter aims to provide guidance on building trust and intimacy in ABDL relationships, helping non-ABDL family members establish open communication and foster an accepting environment.

1. Open Communication: The foundation of building trust and intimacy lies in open and honest communication. Encourage your ABDL loved one to express their feelings, needs, and desires without fear of judgment. Be an active listener, offering empathy and understanding.

2. Respect Boundaries: Boundaries are vital in any relationship, and it is crucial to respect your ABDL loved one's boundaries. Understand their comfort levels and limitations regarding ABDL activities, privacy, and disclosure. Never violate their trust or share personal information without their consent.

3. Educate Yourself: Take the initiative to learn about ABDL identity and its significance. Educating yourself will help you understand your loved one's needs and experiences better. Read books, join online communities, or attend workshops to gain insights and dispel any misconceptions.

4. Empathy and Acceptance: Acceptance is key to fostering a positive environment for your ABDL loved one. Show empathy by putting yourself in

their shoes and trying to understand their experiences and emotions. Avoid judgment and offer support and encouragement.

5. Seek Professional Help if Needed: If you find it challenging to navigate ABDL boundaries or accept your loved one's identity, consider seeking professional help. Therapists or support groups specializing in ABDL relationships can provide guidance and support to both you and your loved one.

6. Promote Positive Intimacy: Intimacy in an ABDL relationship goes beyond physical closeness. It involves emotional connection, trust, and understanding. Encourage positive intimacy by engaging in activities that foster emotional bonding, such as open conversations, shared interests, and mutual respect.

7. Patience and Understanding: Building trust and intimacy takes time. Be patient with your loved one as they navigate their ABDL identity and establish boundaries. Understand that everyone's journey is unique, and your support and understanding are essential.

Remember, building trust and intimacy in ABDL relationships requires ongoing effort and understanding. By following these guidelines, you can establish a healthy and respectful relationship with your ABDL loved one, creating a nurturing environment where trust and intimacy can flourish.

Establishing Emotional Safety and Vulnerability

In any relationship, emotional safety and vulnerability are crucial aspects that pave the way for open communication and a healthy connection. When it comes to navigating the world of ABDL (Adult Baby/Diaper Lover) boundaries, establishing emotional safety and vulnerability becomes even more significant. As a family member of an ABDL individual, it is essential to create a safe space where your loved one can express themselves authentically without fear or judgment.

To begin with, it is vital to educate oneself about ABDL identity and understand that it is a valid and genuine expression of one's self. By seeking knowledge and dispelling any preconceived notions or misconceptions, you can foster empathy and understanding towards your ABDL loved one. This understanding will help you create an environment that acknowledges and accepts their identity.

Once you have familiarized yourself with the ABDL community, it is time to establish open communication. Encourage your loved one to share their thoughts, feelings, and experiences with you. Make it clear that you are there to listen, support, and validate their emotions. By actively listening and responding without judgment, you will enable your loved one to be vulnerable and share their ABDL interests with you.

Creating emotional safety also involves setting boundaries and respecting them. Understand that not all aspects of your loved one's ABDL identity may be comfortable for you to engage with, and that is okay. Communicate your limits and ensure they are respected, just as you should respect your loved one's boundaries. This reciprocal respect will foster trust and emotional safety within the relationship.

In addition to establishing emotional safety, vulnerability is key to building a stronger connection with your ABDL loved one. Allow yourself to be vulnerable by expressing your emotions, concerns, and questions openly. This vulnerability will create a safe space where both of you can learn, grow, and understand each other better.

Remember, establishing emotional safety and vulnerability is an ongoing process. It requires patience, understanding, and a willingness to adapt and learn. By embracing these principles, you can build a healthy and respectful relationship with your ABDL loved one, fostering acceptance, empathy, and a positive environment for everyone involved.

Balancing ABDL Activities with Non-ABDL Relationship Dynamics

When it comes to navigating the intricacies of an ABDL (Adult Baby/Diaper Lover) relationship, finding a balance between ABDL activities and non-ABDL relationship dynamics is crucial. This subchapter aims to guide family members in establishing open communication, setting boundaries, and fostering a healthy and respectful relationship with their ABDL loved one.

Open communication is the foundation of any successful relationship, and this is no different when it comes to ABDL dynamics. It is essential for family members to create a safe space for their loved one to express their needs, desires, and concerns. Encouraging open and non-judgmental dialogue will help foster understanding and empathy between family members and their ABDL loved one.

Setting boundaries is a critical aspect of maintaining a healthy balance between ABDL activities and non-ABDL relationship dynamics. It is important for both parties to communicate their limits and establish mutually agreed-upon guidelines. This may involve discussing the frequency and duration of ABDL activities, as well as identifying specific spaces or times where these activities can take place. By setting clear boundaries, both the ABDL individual and their family members can feel respected and comfortable within the relationship.

In order to achieve acceptance, family members must educate themselves about ABDL identity and strive to understand their loved one's unique experiences. This subchapter offers guidance on cultivating empathy, promoting understanding, and fostering a positive environment. It explores the importance of embracing diversity and recognizing that ABDL identity is a valid and legitimate form of self-expression.

Finally, it is crucial for family members to remember that their loved one's ABDL identity is just one aspect of who they are. It is important to nurture and support their loved one's other interests, hobbies, and relationships outside of the ABDL community. Encouraging a well-rounded life will help maintain a healthy balance between ABDL activities and non-ABDL relationship dynamics.

Navigating the complexities of ABDL relationships can be challenging, but with open communication, established boundaries, acceptance, and support, family members can foster a healthy and respectful relationship with their ABDL loved one. This subchapter provides a comprehensive guide to help family members navigate these boundaries and create an environment where both parties feel understood, accepted, and loved.

Promoting Open Dialogue about Relationship Expectations

In any relationship, open communication is key to establishing trust, understanding, and mutual respect. When it comes to navigating the boundaries of ABDL (Adult Baby Diaper Lover) relationships within a family, it becomes even more crucial to promote open dialogue about relationship expectations. This subchapter aims to provide family members with useful insights and strategies to foster healthy and respectful relationships with their ABDL loved ones.

Understanding and accepting your loved one's ABDL identity is the first step towards open dialogue. It is essential to approach this topic with an open mind, free from judgment or prejudice. Acknowledge that their ABDL identity is a valid part of who they are, and strive to be empathetic and understanding of their needs and desires.

Creating a safe space for open communication is vital. Encourage your loved one to express their thoughts, feelings, and expectations openly. Let them know that you are there to listen and support them. Be patient and non-judgmental, allowing them to open up at their own pace.

Setting clear boundaries is essential for both parties involved. Establishing mutually agreed-upon expectations will help to avoid misunderstandings and conflicts. Encourage your loved one to openly discuss their comfort levels and desires, while also expressing your own boundaries and needs. This open dialogue will allow both parties to negotiate and find a middle ground where both feel respected and valued.

Education plays a crucial role in fostering open communication. Take the time to educate yourself about the ABDL community, its practices, and the reasons behind it. This knowledge will help you approach conversations with a well-informed perspective and avoid making assumptions or generalizations.

Lastly, remember that open dialogue is an ongoing process. Relationships evolve, and so do expectations. Regularly check in with your loved one to ensure that both parties are still comfortable and satisfied with the established boundaries.

By promoting open dialogue about relationship expectations, you are actively contributing to a healthy and respectful relationship with your ABDL loved one. Through empathy, understanding, and a willingness to learn, you can create an environment that fosters acceptance and supports their ABDL identity. Remember, love knows no boundaries, and with open dialogue, you can build bridges of understanding and strengthen your familial bond.

Addressing Challenges and Conflicts in ABDL Relationships

Introduction:
In any relationship, challenges and conflicts are inevitable. When it comes to ABDL (Adult Baby/Diaper Lover) relationships, these challenges can be unique and require special attention. This subchapter aims to provide guidance to family members of ABDL individuals on how to address and navigate the challenges and conflicts that may arise in their relationships.

Understanding ABDL Identity:
Before addressing the challenges, it is essential for family members to have a basic understanding of the ABDL identity. ABDL individuals find comfort and fulfillment in regressing to a childlike state or expressing their affection for diapers. It is crucial to approach this identity with empathy, openness, and a willingness to learn.

Open Communication:
Maintaining open communication is vital in any relationship, and ABDL relationships are no exception. Encourage your loved one to express their feelings, desires, and concerns without fear of judgment. Create a safe space where they feel comfortable discussing their ABDL identity and needs. By fostering open communication, you can address conflicts more effectively and find solutions that work for both parties.

Respecting Boundaries:
Respecting boundaries is crucial in any relationship, and ABDL relationships are built on trust and consent. Understand and acknowledge the boundaries set by your ABDL loved one. Respect their choice to engage in ABDL activities privately or within a specific space. It is essential to establish clear boundaries and ensure that all family members are aware of them to avoid potential conflicts.

Education and Empathy:
Educating yourself about ABDL identity and experiences is key to fostering empathy and understanding. By learning more about ABDL culture, you can better appreciate the motivations and emotions behind your loved one's choices. Show empathy by actively listening, asking questions, and seeking to understand their perspective. This will contribute to a positive and accepting family environment.

Seeking Support:
Addressing challenges and conflicts alone can be overwhelming. Seek support from ABDL communities, therapists, or support groups specializing in ABDL

relationships. Connecting with others who have similar experiences can provide valuable insights, advice, and emotional support.

Conclusion:
Addressing challenges and conflicts in ABDL relationships requires open communication, respect for boundaries, empathy, and a willingness to learn. By embracing these principles, family members can foster healthy, respectful relationships with their ABDL loved ones. Remember, acceptance and understanding are the foundations of a positive family environment where everyone's needs are acknowledged and respected.

Coping with Intimacy Issues and Emotional Challenges

Intimacy is an essential aspect of any relationship, and it can present unique challenges when one partner identifies as an Adult Baby/Diaper Lover (ABDL). As a family member, it is important to understand and navigate these intimacy issues and emotional challenges to ensure a healthy and respectful relationship with your ABDL loved one. This subchapter aims to provide guidance on how to address these issues and foster open communication.

Intimacy can be a sensitive topic for individuals in the ABDL community due to the vulnerability and trust required. As a family member, it is crucial to approach this subject with empathy and understanding. Recognize that your loved one's ABDL identity is an integral part of who they are, and their desires for intimacy may differ from societal norms. Open communication is key to navigating these differences. Encourage your loved one to express their needs and desires, and make them feel safe to share their vulnerabilities with you.

It is essential to establish boundaries regarding intimacy within the context of the ABDL lifestyle. Understand the boundaries that your loved one has set for themselves and respect them. If you have any concerns or questions, approach them in a non-judgmental and supportive manner. Remember that consent and mutual agreement are crucial in any intimate relationship, and this holds true for ABDL relationships as well.

Emotional challenges may arise when a family member struggles to accept their loved one's ABDL identity. It is important to approach this situation with empathy and an open mind. Educate yourself about the ABDL community to gain a deeper understanding of your loved one's experiences. Offer your support and reassurance, letting them know that you are there for them without judgment.

Creating a positive environment for your loved one is key to fostering acceptance. Encourage open dialogue within the family to address any concerns or misunderstandings. Seek professional help if needed, such as therapy or support groups, to gain further insights into the ABDL community and navigate emotional challenges effectively.

Remember, the journey to acceptance and understanding may take time. Be patient with yourself and your loved one as you navigate these intimate and emotional challenges together. By fostering a healthy and respectful relationship, you can create an environment where your loved one feels loved, accepted, and understood for who they truly are.

Resolving Differences in ABDL and Non-ABDL Interests

One of the challenges that family members often face when a loved one embraces an ABDL (Adult Baby/Diaper Lover) identity is navigating the differences in interests and preferences. This subchapter aims to provide guidance on how to resolve these differences and establish open communication, ensuring a healthy and respectful relationship with your ABDL loved one.

First and foremost, it is essential to approach these differences with empathy and understanding. Remember that your loved one's ABDL identity is a significant part of who they are, and acceptance is crucial for their emotional well-being. Acknowledge that their interests may be different from yours, but that doesn't diminish their value or worth as an individual.

Open communication is the cornerstone of any healthy relationship, and when it comes to bridging the gap between ABDL and non-ABDL interests, it becomes even more critical. Take the initiative to have honest and non-judgmental conversations with your loved one. Ask them about their ABDL interests, why it is important to them, and how they would like you to be involved or supportive.

It is essential to set boundaries that work for both parties involved. Discuss what activities or behaviors are comfortable for you and which ones may make you feel uneasy or conflicted. This dialogue will help establish a common ground where both your interests and your loved one's ABDL interests can coexist harmoniously.

Education plays a vital role in resolving differences. Educate yourself about ABDL culture, terminology, and the reasons behind it. This knowledge will help you understand your loved one's perspective better, allowing you to approach the situation with empathy and compassion. It will also enable you to dispel any misconceptions or stereotypes you may have had about ABDL.

Seeking professional guidance can be incredibly beneficial for both you and your loved one. A therapist or counselor experienced in dealing with ABDL-related issues can provide a safe space for open communication, offer guidance on navigating differences, and help you both explore ways to foster a positive and respectful environment.

Remember, resolving differences in ABDL and non-ABDL interests requires patience, understanding, and a willingness to learn and grow together. By embracing open communication, setting boundaries, educating yourself, and seeking professional support, you can create a strong foundation for a healthy and loving relationship with your ABDL loved one.

Seeking Couples Counseling for ABDL Relationship Dynamics

In any relationship, it is natural to encounter challenges and dynamics that require open communication and understanding. When one partner identifies as Adult Baby/Diaper Lover (ABDL), it can introduce unique complexities that may test the boundaries and understanding of both partners. Seeking couples counseling can be a valuable resource for navigating these dynamics and fostering a healthy and respectful relationship.

Couples counseling provides a safe space for both partners to express their feelings, concerns, and needs. It offers a platform for non-ABDL family members to understand their loved one's ABDL identity better, fostering empathy and acceptance. By engaging in therapy together, both partners can gain insights into each other's perspectives and work towards establishing open communication.

For non-ABDL family members, couples counseling can help navigate the boundaries that may arise in an ABDL relationship. It offers guidance on setting and respecting personal boundaries, ensuring that both partners feel comfortable and secure in their relationship. Through therapy, family members can learn about the ABDL community, its significance to their loved one, and ways to support their partner while maintaining their own boundaries.

Couples counseling can also assist in addressing any concerns or misconceptions that non-ABDL family members may have about their loved one's ABDL identity. It provides a platform for open dialogue, fostering understanding and acceptance. Therapists can guide family members in exploring their emotions, helping them process any feelings of discomfort or confusion they may experience.

Furthermore, seeking couples counseling for ABDL relationship dynamics can help partners develop strategies for creating a positive environment. Therapists can offer guidance on fostering intimacy, trust, and respect, ensuring that both partners feel valued and supported. They can help couples establish effective communication channels, enabling them to express their needs and desires in a healthy and constructive manner.

In conclusion, couples counseling can be an invaluable resource for non-ABDL family members navigating the boundaries of an ABDL relationship. It provides a platform for open communication, empathy, and understanding. By seeking therapy together, partners can work towards establishing a healthy and respectful relationship, fostering acceptance, and creating a positive environment for both individuals to thrive.

Celebrating and Embracing ABDL as a Part of Your Loved One's Identity

Understanding and accepting the ABDL (Adult Baby/Diaper Lover) identity of your loved one can be challenging. However, it is essential to navigate this aspect of their life with empathy, respect, and open communication. In this chapter, we will explore ways to celebrate and embrace ABDL as a part of your loved one's identity, fostering a healthy and inclusive environment.

Firstly, it is crucial to educate yourself about ABDL. By learning more about this community, you will gain a deeper understanding of your loved one's needs, desires, and motivations. Engage in open conversations with them, allowing them to share their experiences and feelings. This will help foster trust and build a stronger connection.

Embracing your loved one's ABDL identity requires empathy. It is essential to acknowledge that their desires and interests are valid and should be respected. Avoid shaming or judging them based on societal norms or personal biases. Remember, their ABDL identity is an integral part of who they are, and by accepting it, you can create a more loving and supportive environment.

Another vital aspect of celebrating ABDL as a part of your loved one's identity is setting boundaries. Openly discuss their needs and expectations, as well as your own. Establishing clear boundaries will help both parties feel comfortable and safe within the relationship. This might include discussions about when and where ABDL activities are appropriate and how they can be integrated into your lives without compromising anyone's comfort.

Creating a positive environment is key to fostering acceptance. Encourage open and non-judgmental communication within your family. By maintaining a safe space for discussions, your loved one will feel more comfortable sharing their thoughts and experiences. Remember to be patient and understanding, as acceptance may take time for some family members.

Seeking support from like-minded communities or professionals can also be beneficial. Connecting with other family members who have embraced their loved one's ABDL identity can provide guidance, advice, and a sense of belonging. Therapists or counselors who specialize in alternative lifestyles can also offer valuable insights and strategies for navigating this aspect of your loved one's identity.

In conclusion, celebrating and embracing ABDL as a part of your loved one's identity requires empathy, understanding, and open communication. Educate yourself, set boundaries, and create a positive environment for discussions. Remember, acceptance may take time, but by fostering a healthy and respectful relationship, you can strengthen your bond with your loved one and truly celebrate all aspects of their identity.

Embracing ABDL Activities and Rituals within the Relationship

In this subchapter, we will explore the importance of embracing ABDL activities and rituals within the relationship with your ABDL loved one. By understanding the significance of these activities and rituals, you can foster a healthy and respectful relationship while supporting their ABDL identity.

ABDL activities and rituals are an integral part of your loved one's ABDL lifestyle. These activities can include wearing diapers, using pacifiers, engaging in age regression play, and participating in caregiver dynamics. For those who may be unfamiliar with ABDL, understanding the reasons behind these activities is crucial.

First and foremost, it is essential to recognize that ABDL activities and rituals are not inherently sexual. They serve as a form of self-expression and comfort for individuals who identify as ABDL. These activities provide a sense of security, stress relief, and emotional connection. By participating in these activities, your loved one can experience a sense of freedom and acceptance.

To embrace ABDL activities and rituals, it is vital to establish open communication and set clear boundaries. Talk openly about your loved one's desires, expectations, and comfort levels. Ask questions and listen attentively to their needs. This will allow you to better understand the significance of these activities and how they contribute to their emotional well-being.

Creating a positive environment is key in supporting your loved one's ABDL identity. Avoid judgment or stigmatization. Instead, focus on empathy and understanding. Educate yourself about ABDL and engage in open-minded discussions. This will help to dispel any misconceptions and foster acceptance within the family.

Participating in ABDL activities and rituals can be a bonding experience for both you and your loved one. If you feel comfortable, engage in age regression play or caregiver dynamics. This can help strengthen the emotional connection and trust between you. Remember, these activities are consensual and should always be practiced in a safe and respectful manner.

Lastly, be mindful of privacy and confidentiality. ABDL activities and rituals are personal and private experiences. Respect your loved one's boundaries and ensure that their privacy is protected. Openly discuss any concerns or questions you may have, but always prioritize their comfort and well-being.

By embracing ABDL activities and rituals within the relationship, you are demonstrating your love and acceptance for your ABDL loved one. Through open communication, empathy, and understanding, you can create a safe and supportive environment that fosters a healthy and respectful relationship for both of you.

Participating in ABDL Events and Celebrations

Introduction:

Participating in ABDL events and celebrations can be a wonderful way for family members to support their loved ones who identify as ABDL (Adult Baby Diaper Lover). These events provide a safe and inclusive space where ABDL individuals can connect with others who share similar interests, form friendships, and celebrate their unique identities. This subchapter aims to guide family members on how to navigate these events, foster open communication, and establish a healthy and respectful relationship with their ABDL loved one.

Understanding ABDL Events:

ABDL events range from local meetups to larger conventions, parties, and gatherings. These events offer a variety of activities, such as workshops, socializing, and themed parties, all centered around the ABDL community. It is important for family members to educate themselves about these events to gain a better understanding of what their loved one may experience and what to expect.

Supporting Your Loved One:

Attending ABDL events with your loved one can demonstrate your support and acceptance of their identity. Before attending, have an open and honest conversation to understand their expectations, boundaries, and any concerns they may have. It is crucial to respect their wishes and honor their privacy during these events.

Communication and Boundaries:

Maintaining open communication is key to a healthy relationship with your ABDL loved one. Discuss boundaries and expectations beforehand. Allow them to express their needs, concerns, and desires for privacy during events. Establishing clear boundaries will help create a safe and comfortable environment for both of you.

Embracing Acceptance:

If you are struggling with accepting your loved one's ABDL identity, attending these events can be an opportunity for growth and understanding. Take the time to engage with other ABDL individuals and their families, listen to their stories, and gain insight into their experiences. Fostering empathy and understanding will help create a positive environment for your loved one to feel accepted and loved.

Conclusion:

Participating in ABDL events and celebrations can be a valuable experience for family members. By educating yourself about these events, supporting your loved one, maintaining open communication, and embracing acceptance, you can establish a healthy and respectful relationship with your ABDL family member. Remember, the key is to approach these events with love, understanding, and a willingness to learn.

Supporting Your Loved One's ABDL Journey and Growth

Introduction:

When a family member reveals their ABDL (Adult Baby/Diaper Lover) identity, it can be challenging for non-ABDL family members to understand and navigate this new territory. This subchapter aims to provide guidance and support for family members as they embark on this journey alongside their loved one. By establishing open communication, respecting boundaries, and fostering a positive environment, we can ensure a healthy and respectful relationship with our ABDL family member.

Establishing Open Communication:

The first step in supporting your loved one's ABDL journey is to establish open and honest communication. Create a safe space where they feel comfortable sharing their thoughts, feelings, and experiences without fear of judgment. Listen with empathy, seeking to understand their perspective and validate their feelings. Encourage open dialogue and ask questions to gain a better understanding of their ABDL identity.

Respecting Boundaries:

Respecting boundaries is crucial in maintaining a healthy relationship with your ABDL loved one. Understand that they may have specific preferences regarding their ABDL activities and lifestyle. Take the time to discuss and establish boundaries together to ensure both parties feel comfortable and respected. Remember that boundaries can evolve over time, so ongoing communication is essential.

Fostering a Positive Environment:

Creating a positive environment is essential for your loved one's ABDL journey and growth. Educate yourself about ABDL culture, terminology, and the positive aspects it brings to their life. Celebrate their identity and show support through small gestures like acknowledging their achievements, providing space for ABDL-related activities, or offering to accompany them to

ABDL events or meetups. By fostering a positive environment, you can strengthen your relationship and promote acceptance.

Seeking External Support:

Navigating your loved one's ABDL journey may feel overwhelming at times. Remember that seeking external support can be beneficial for both you and your loved one. Consider joining support groups or online communities specifically geared towards non-ABDL family members. These groups provide a safe space to share experiences, seek advice, and gain a better understanding of ABDL dynamics.

Conclusion:

Supporting your loved one's ABDL journey and growth requires open communication, respect for boundaries, and fostering a positive environment. By embracing empathy, understanding, and acceptance, you can strengthen your relationship and ensure a healthy and respectful connection with your ABDL loved one. Remember, this journey is about love, acceptance, and growth, and with the right support, you can create a harmonious and inclusive family environment for all.

Conclusion: Embracing Love and Acceptance in ABDL Relationships

In this final chapter, we have explored the intricacies of ABDL relationships and the importance of establishing healthy boundaries and open communication. Throughout this guide, our aim has been to provide family members with the tools and understanding necessary to foster a loving and accepting environment for their ABDL loved ones.

One of the key takeaways from our discussion is the significance of empathy and understanding. It is essential for family members to recognize that ABDL identities are a valid expression of self and should be respected. By embracing love and acceptance, we can bridge the gap between the non-ABDL family members and their ABDL loved ones.

Communication plays a pivotal role in any relationship, and ABDL relationships are no exception. We have emphasized the importance of establishing open lines of communication, where both parties feel comfortable discussing their needs, concerns, and boundaries. By fostering a safe space for dialogue, non-ABDL family members can better understand the motivations and desires behind their loved one's ABDL identity.

Furthermore, we have explored the significance of setting boundaries. Boundaries are not meant to restrict or judge, but rather to establish mutual respect and understanding within the relationship. Understanding each other's limits and comfort levels is crucial for maintaining a healthy and loving dynamic.

It is important to remember that embracing love and acceptance does not mean that non-ABDL family members need to participate in the ABDL lifestyle themselves. Acceptance is about recognizing and supporting their loved one's identity without judgment or prejudice. By acknowledging and validating their ABDL loved one's experiences, non-ABDL family members can play a significant role in their overall happiness and well-being.

Lastly, we would like to emphasize the significance of continued learning and growth. ABDL relationships may be unfamiliar territory for many non-ABDL family members, but with an open mind and a willingness to understand, we can foster an environment of love, acceptance, and support.

In conclusion, navigating ABDL boundaries and embracing love and acceptance in ABDL relationships is a journey that requires compassion, understanding, and open communication. By following the guidance provided in this guide, non-ABDL family members can build strong, respectful, and loving relationships with their ABDL loved ones. Remember, love knows no bounds, and by embracing acceptance, we can create a harmonious and fulfilling life together.

www.ingramcontent.com/pod-product-compliance
Lightning Source LLC
Chambersburg PA
CBHW070821280726
48660CB00017B/2386